atxh sitee

Ts'idāne dege lēgūt'ē

Xwexwéyt re Stsmémelt

Enso Binoojiinh Piitendaagzi

ᒪᐦᓯ ᐊᐧᐋᐧᐣ ᐃᐣᐱᐦᐠᑳᒋᐦᐃᒋᑯᐤ

ᓴᑭᒋᐦᐃᐧᐁᐧᐣ ᐱᓯᒋᑫᐧᐊᐧᐠ

Kahkiiyow Lii Zaanfaan akishoowuk

U, XÁXE MEQ TŦE SȾELIȾḴEⱢ Every Child Matters

wə x̌iʔ tə steʔəx̌ʷəɬ tə məḱʷ wet

tahto awāsis ispihtēyihtākosiw

Łdakát adátx'i atxh sitee

Ts'idāne dege lēgūt'ē

Xwexwéyt re Stsmémelt

Enso Binoojiinh Piitendaagzi

ᒪᐦᓯ ᐊᐧᐋᐧᐣ ᐃᐣᐱᐦᐠᑳᒋᐦᐃᒋᑯᐤ

ᓴᑭᒋᐦᐃᐧᐁᐧᐣ ᐱᓯᒋᑫᐧᐊᐧᐠ

Kahkiiyow Lii Zaanfaan akishoowuk

U, XÁXE MEQ TŦE SȾELIȾḴEⱢ Every Child Matters

wə x̌iʔ tə steʔəx̌ʷəɬ tə məḱʷ wet

I dedicate this book to my Grandmother, Lena Jack, who had no choice in her 10 children attending Residential School. I cannot imagine the pain of having your children taken away and not be able to do anything about it. Granny was always a pillar of strength for our family, our matriarch and someone that we will always miss dearly.

This book is in remembrance of you.

~ Phyllis Webstad

I dedicate this book to my late Uncle Victor, who was forced to attend Kamloops Indian Residential School. He was a hunter, a language speaker and a loving uncle to all of his nieces and nephews. His spirit lives on with his younger kin who continue to fish, hunt, sing, and thrive on the land.

~ Karlene Harvey

Canada Based Toll-Free Help Lines
24-hour National Indian Residential School crisis line — 1-866-925-4419
Indigenous Hope for Wellness Helpline — 1-855-242-3310
Kids Help Phone — 1-800-668-6868
Suicide Prevention and Support — 1-833-456-4566
9-1-1 Emergency

EVERY CHILD MATTERS

Phyllis Webstad

Karlene Harvey

Since time immemorial, Indigenous Peoples have lived on Turtle Island
celebrating, practicing and honoring our own Indigenous cultures.

Since time immemorial...

our dances have been danced.

our songs have been sung.

Łdakát adátx'i atxh sitee

Ts'ídāne dege lēgūt'ē

Xwexwéyt re Stsmémelt

ᒐᐧᑐ ᐊᐊᐧᐦ·ᕐ ᐃᐣᐱᐦᐅᐸᐦᒼᐧᐧᑯᕈᐧ

Enso Binoojiinh Piitendaagzi

ᓱᐱᑯᒪᑕᐧ ᐱᐧᒪᓇᐃᐧᐧ

Kahkiiyow Lii Zaanfaan akishoowuk

U, X̱ÁX̱E MEQ TᵻE S̱TELITḴEⱢ

wə ƛ̓i? tə steʔəx̌ʷəɬ tə mək̓ʷ wet

tahto awāsis ispihtēyihtākosiw

our languages have been spoken.

Since time immemorial...

our teachings have been honoured.

our ceremonies have been loved.

our cultures have been practiced.

our families have been together.

For many years, Indigenous Peoples have been told that our way of life is wrong and that we should change who we are. A system was created to stop us from being who we were meant to be — Indigenous Peoples. It was called the Residential School System.

Because of Residential Schools, thousands of Indigenous children...

were made to leave their homes and families.

were forced to stop speaking their language.

At Residential School, thousands of Indigenous children...

were stripped of their identity.

felt afraid and alone — like they did not matter.

At Residential School...

our dances were banned.

our songs were silenced.

our languages were quieted.

our teachings were stripped.

our ceremonies were attacked.

our cultures were shamed.

our children were taken.

My name is Phyllis, and I am one of these children.

When I was six-years-old, my Granny bought me a brand new orange shirt for my first day of school. I wore my orange shirt with excitement. I got on the bus and I was taken to a Residential School two hours away from my home and family.

My hair was cut.
I could not live with my family.
I felt alone and confused.
I felt unloved and uncared for.
No one explained why I could not go home.
It was a very difficult time.
I felt like I did not matter.

After 300 sleeps, I finally went home.
Thousands of children were not as lucky as me.
For a long time, I believed I did not matter;
and I was not the only one.

Today, I know that it is not true.

Now I know I have the right to
walk on this earth and breathe this
air as much as anyone else.

Nobody is better or less than me.

I matter.

Even with Residential Schools in our history, we will continue to...

dance our dances.

Xwexwéyt re Stsmémelt

sing our songs.

speak our languages.

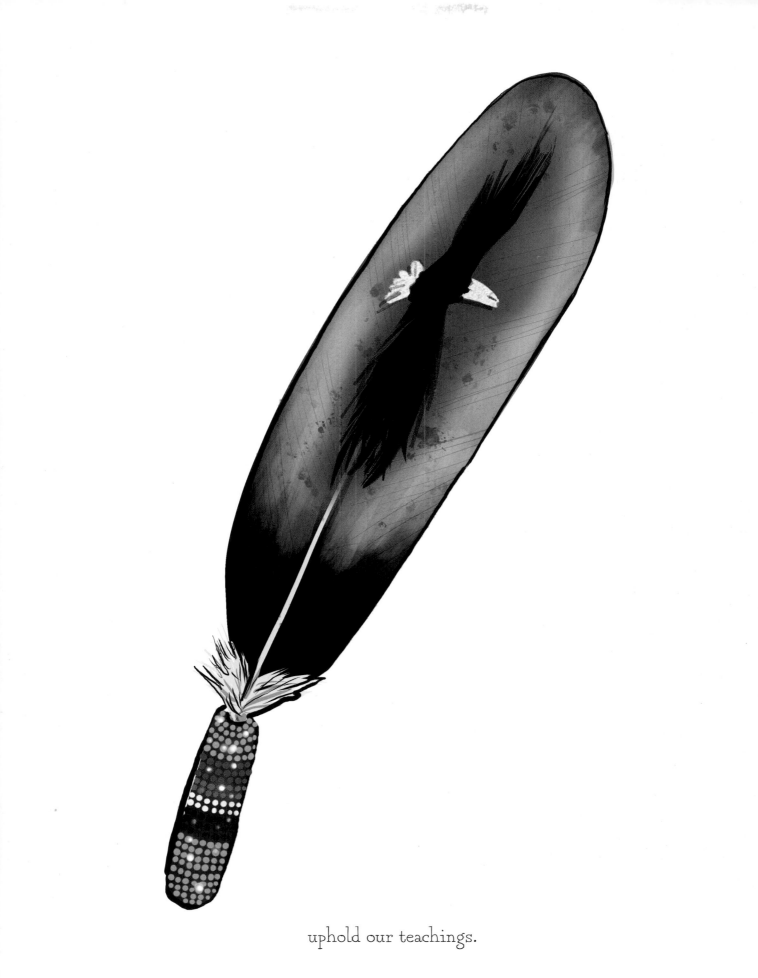

uphold our teachings.

Even with Residential Schools in our history, we will continue to...

love our ceremonies.

practice our cultures.

and keep our families united.

We remain strong. We remain resilient. We Survived.

We matter.

Every Child Matters.

If you are a Survivor of Residential School ...

You Matter

If you are a family member of a Residential School Survivor...

You Matter

For the children who didn't come home...

You
Matter

The child inside each and every one of us matters.

You Matter

No matter what colour on the medicine wheel you are, you matter.
Every Child Matters in the past, the present, and the future.

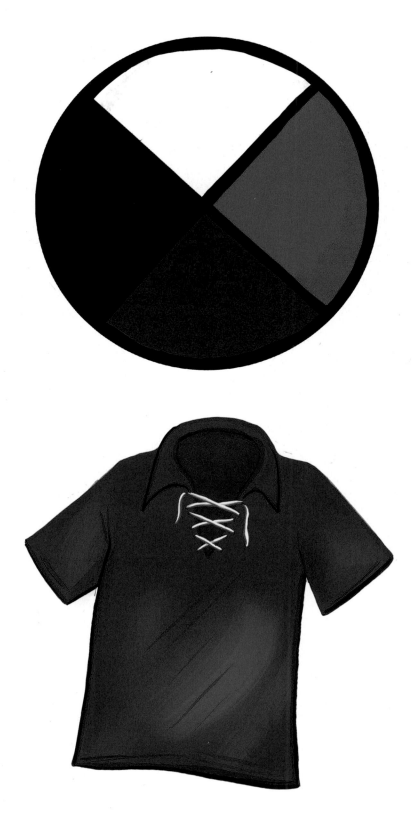

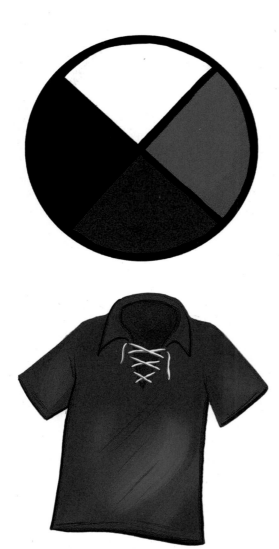

Glossary

Every Child Matters in some Indigenous Languages.

Xwexwéyt re Stsmémelt	Secwépemc
Łdakát adátx'i atxh sitee	Lingít (Tlingit)
Ts'ídāne dege lēgūt'ē	Kaska
tahto awāsis ispihtēyihtākosiw	Cree
ᑕᐦᑐ ᐊᐋᐧᓯᐢ ᐃᐢᐱᐦᑌᔨᐦᑖᑯᓯᐤ	Cree
Enso Binoojiinh Piitendaagzi	Ojibway
Kahkiiyow Lii Zaanfaan akishoowuk	Southern Michif
wə ƛ̓iʔ tə steʔəxʷəɬ tə mək̓ʷ wet	Hәn̓q̓әmin̓әm̓ (Musqueam)
ᓱᕈᓯᓕᒫᑦ ᐱᒻᒪᕆᐅᔪᑦ	Inuktitut, Northern Baffin dialect
U, XÁXE MEQ TŦE ST**ELI**T**K**E**Ł**	SENĆOŦEN

Medicine Wheel Publishing has sourced these translations from Indigenous language speakers or legitimate sources that have used them in their publications or organizations. We acknowledge that within Indigenous languages, there may be different variations of spelling and even perspectives on how to translate 'Every Child Matters'. We would like to acknowledge there are many other Indigenous languages that were not included in this book.

Thank you to everyone who offered their help.

Also by Phyllis Webstad

With Our Orange Hearts
English | French — Ages 3-5
Illustrated by Emily Kewageshig
Best-selling children's book in
Canada in September 2022

Phyllis's Orange Shirt
English | French — Ages 4-6
BC Best Seller in September 2019

The Orange Shirt Story
English | French | Shuswap — Ages 7+
Best-selling children's book in Canada
in September 2018

Beyond the Orange Shirt Story
English | French — Ages 16+
BC Best Seller September 2021

 Canada Council
for the Arts

Conseil des arts
du Canada

 Funded by the
Government
of Canada

Financé par le
gouvernement
du Canada

 Canadä

 BRITISH COLUMBIA
ARTS COUNCIL

BRITISH
COLUMBIA

Supported by the Province of British Columbia

Every
Child
Matters

ᑕᐦᑐ ᐊᐚᓯᐢ
ᐃᐢᐱᐦᑌᔨᐦᑖᑯᓯᐤ

tahto awāsis ispihtēyihtākosiw

Łdakát adátx'i
atxh sitee

Ts'ídāne
dege
lēgūt'ē

Xwexwéyt re
Stsmémelt

Enso Binoojiinh
Piitendaagzi

ᓱᕈᓯᑕᒫᑦ
ᐱᒻᒪᕆᐅᔪᑦ

Kahkiiyow
Lii Zaanfaan
akishoowuk

U, XÁXE
MEQ TŦE
S<u>T</u>ELIT<u>K</u>EŁ

wə ƛ̓i? tə
ste?əxʷəɬ
tə mək̓ʷ wet

Every
Child
Matters

ᑕᐦᑐ ᐊᐚᓯᐢ
ᐃᐢᐱᐦᑌᔨᐦᑖᑯᓯᐤ

tahto awāsis ispihtēyihtākosiw

Łdakát adátx'i
atxh sitee

Ts'ídāne
dege
lēgūt'ē

Xwexwéyt re
Stsmémelt

Enso Binoojiinh
Piitendaagzi

ᓱᕈᓯᑕᒫᑦ
ᐱᒻᒪᕆᐅᔪᑦ

Kahkiiyow
Lii Zaanfaan
akishoowuk

U, XÁXE
MEQ TŦE
S<u>T</u>ELIT<u>K</u>EŁ

wə ƛ̓i? tə
ste?əxʷəɬ
tə mək̓ʷ wet